My Everyday Life

written by
Latisha Jefferson-Robertson

For everyone learning to honor their life exactly as it is — especially when the world asks them to move faster than their body allows or their health and spirit can afford.

MY EVERYDAY LIFE

Written By
Latisha Jefferson-Robertson

Cover Image By
Tisha Ann

Fullcover Design By
Sun Child Wind Spirit

Proofread By
Ukirah Yasmine

Edited By
Mylia Tiye Mal Jaza

My Everyday Life
Copyright © 2026, Latisha Jefferson-Robertson
All Rights Reserved.

Softback ISBN 10: 4225015653
Softback ISBN 13: 9781847304292

This art is a book of non-fiction. No part of this work may be reproduced or transmitted in any form or by any means (graphic, electronic, magnetic, photographic, or mechanical - including photocopying, recording, taping, or by any information storage/retrieval system) without the written permission of the author/publisher. Post demise of author/ publisher, then valid permission for reproduction and transmittal must be obtained from multiple immediate/major survivors of the author's family. Although careful preparation of this work permeated every phase, it is understood that perfection is humanly impossible. Further, the content of this book does not serve as professional counseling. Thus, neither the self-publishing associate, author/publisher nor imprinter accepts liability for errors, omissions, nor damages resulting from the use of any information presented herein.

<u>Author</u>
Latisha Ann Jefferson-Robertson
latishajefferson2@gmail.com
Facebook.com/Sweetdivine.Mustshine

<u>*Self-Publishing Associate*</u>
Dr. Mary M. Jefferson
BePublished.Org - Chicago, IL
(972) 880-8316
www.bepublished.org

First Edition.
Printed In the USA
Recycled Paper Encouraged.

Table of Contents

Part I: The Quiet Beginnings 8

    Chapter 1: Morning Thoughts 9

    Chapter 2 Life Behind Closed Doors 15

    Chapter 3 The Woman in the Mirror 20

    Chapter 4 Lessons I Learned the Hard Way 26

Part II: Everyday Realities 31

    Chapter 5 Balancing It All 32

    Chapter 6 Love, Family, and Expectations 37

    Chapter 7 The Weight I Carry Silently 42

    Chapter 8 Strength in Routine 47

Part III: Growth & Reflection 52

    Chapter 9 Healing in My Own Time 53

    Chapter 10 When I Chose Myself 58

(more)

TOC *(cont'd)*

    Chapter 11 Faith, Hope, and Resilience 63

    Chapter 12 Becoming More Than I Was 68

Part IV: Looking Forward 72

    Chapter 13 Gratitude in Small Moments 73

    Chapter 14 Redefining My Everyday Life 77

Closing Reflections 81

    ESSAY - Learning To Be Me Again 82

    POEM - Still Becoming 91

The Art & Artist 95

(###)

Part I
The Quiet Beginnings

Chapter 1
Morning Thoughts

Mornings have always spoken to me in a quiet language. Before the world wakes up fully—before phones start ringing, responsibilities start calling, and expectations start pressing—I find myself alone with my thoughts. These early moments belong only to me. They are the few minutes when life hasn't yet decided what it wants from me, and I can simply exist.

I wake up most mornings before the sun finishes rising. Not because I have to, but because my mind refuses to stay asleep. Years of living, worrying, hoping, and surviving have trained it to be alert early. I lie still for a moment, staring at the ceiling, listening to the house breathe. There's something comforting about that silence. It reminds me that even in a busy life, stillness is possible.

As an African American woman, my mornings often begin with more than just stretching and brushing my teeth. They begin with preparation—mental, emotional, and sometimes spiritual. The world doesn't

MY EVERYDAY LIFE

always make room for softness in women like me, so I've learned to create that space for myself. In these early hours, I gather my strength before stepping into a day that may ask more of me than I feel ready to give.

I sit at the edge of my bed and let my feet touch the floor. That simple act grounds me. It reminds me that I'm here, that I made it through another day and another night. Some mornings, gratitude comes easily. Other mornings, it feels forced, like a habit I'm trying to relearn. But I remind myself that waking up is already a victory, even when I don't feel victorious.

My thoughts wander as I move through my morning routine. I think about where I am in life and how I got here. I think about the younger version of myself—the girl who believed life would look a certain way by now. I wonder what she would say if she could see me today. Would she be proud of my resilience, or disappointed that some dreams had to change shape? I try not to judge myself too harshly. Life has a way of teaching lessons that no one prepares you for.

In the mirror, I see a woman shaped by experience. My face tells stories my mouth doesn't always share. There are lines that weren't there years ago, signs of stress, laughter, and quiet endurance. I've learned to study my reflection without flinching. This face has carried me through joy and heartbreak. It has smiled when it didn't feel like smiling and held tears back when crying didn't feel safe.

Some mornings, my reflection feels familiar. Other mornings, it feels like I'm looking at someone still becoming. I've realized that becoming doesn't stop at a certain age. It doesn't end when you reach milestones or check boxes off a list. Becoming is ongoing, especially for women who have had to be strong longer than they should have.

As I make my coffee or tea, the warmth of the cup between my hands feels grounding. It's one of the few rituals I've managed to keep consistent. Life changes quickly—jobs, relationships, priorities—but this small routine remains. It reminds me that stability doesn't always come in big forms. Sometimes it's found in the simple, repeated acts that anchor us.

My mornings are also when I do my most honest thinking. I replay conversations from the past, imagine how I could have spoken up differently, wonder if I was too quiet or too loud. I think about the roles I play—

daughter, mother, friend, worker, caregiver—and how easy it is to lose myself beneath them. I ask myself questions I don't always answer out loud: Am I happy? Am I fulfilled? Am I living for myself or just surviving for others?

These thoughts don't always have neat conclusions. Sometimes they linger all day. But acknowledging them feels important. For a long time, I pushed my thoughts aside to keep things moving. There was always something that needed to be done, someone who needed me. But ignoring yourself has a cost. I've learned that the quiet moments demand honesty, whether you're ready for it or not.

Being an African American woman has shaped my mornings in ways I didn't always recognize at first. There's an unspoken awareness that follows me into each day—a knowledge of how the world may see me before it hears me. I prepare myself to be misunderstood, underestimated, or expected to be strong without question. That awareness can be heavy, but it's also made me observant, thoughtful, and deeply reflective.

Still, I don't want my mornings to be defined only by what I'm bracing myself against. I want them to be moments of intention. So I try to speak kindness into my day before the noise begins. Some mornings I whisper affirmations, other mornings I just breathe deeply and sit in the quiet. Both are enough.

I've learned that mornings are less about productivity and more about presence. The world pushes us to rush, to do, to prove. But the mornings remind me that simply being is valuable too. That my worth isn't measured by how much I accomplish before noon.

As the day begins to unfold, sounds slowly fill the space—cars passing, voices rising, life moving forward. I take one last moment before stepping fully into it. I remind myself that I don't have to have everything figured out today. That it's okay to move slowly, to feel deeply, to take up space as I am.

Morning thoughts don't always bring clarity, but they offer something just as important: connection. Connection to myself, to my history, and to the woman I'm still becoming. They remind me that my everyday life—ordinary as it may seem—is filled with meaning, reflection, and quiet strength.

MY EVERYDAY LIFE

And so I begin the day, carrying those thoughts with me. Not as burdens, but as reminders that my story matters, even in its simplest moments.

Chapter 2
Life Behind Closed Doors

There is a version of my life that the world sees, and then there is the life that exists behind closed doors. The difference between the two is quiet but significant. Outside, I am composed, capable, and dependable. Inside my home, where no one is watching, I allow myself to exhale. This is where the truth lives—not polished, not filtered, just real.

Behind closed doors, I am not performing strength. I am resting from it.

For a long time, I didn't realize how much energy it took to show up as "okay." I thought that was just part of being an adult, part of being a woman, part of being an African American woman who learned early on that vulnerability was a luxury. The world often expects us to carry more, complain less, and keep moving no matter what weighs us down. So I did. Day after day. Smile after smile.

But when the door closes and the locks click into place, something shifts. My shoulders drop. My face

MY EVERYDAY LIFE

relaxes. The version of me that doesn't need to explain herself finally gets to breathe.

Home is where I confront the parts of myself I don't always understand. It's where emotions surface that I didn't have time to feel earlier. Some evenings, that means silence. Other nights, it means tears that come without warning. I've learned not to judge those moments. They are evidence that I am human, not weak.

There were times in my life when home didn't feel safe emotionally. Times when the walls heard arguments, disappointments, and unspoken pain. Those memories still linger, even now. Sometimes I'll catch myself bracing for conflict that never comes, reacting to echoes of old experiences. Healing, I've learned, doesn't erase the past—it teaches you how to live with it gently.

Behind closed doors is also where I question myself the most. Did I say the right thing today? Did I let something slide that I shouldn't have? Am I being fair to myself, or am I holding myself to impossible standards? These questions don't always demand answers, but they remind me that reflection is part of growth.

I've noticed that I'm hardest on myself in private. In public, I give grace freely. I understand others' mistakes, offer compassion, extend patience. But alone, I replay my missteps like scenes from a movie I can't turn off. Learning to treat myself with the same kindness I give others has been one of my greatest challenges.

There is also joy behind closed doors—quiet joy that doesn't need an audience. Dancing in the kitchen to music that understands me. Laughing at something small and silly. Sitting in comfortable silence, wrapped in a blanket, feeling safe enough to do nothing at all. These moments may seem insignificant, but they restore me in ways the outside world never could.

As an African American woman, privacy has always been sacred to me. There's a long history of our lives being scrutinized, misunderstood, and judged. Having a space where I can exist freely—without explanation or defense—is something I cherish deeply. Behind closed doors, I am not defined by stereotypes or expectations. I am simply myself.

This is also where I grieve quietly. Loss doesn't always announce itself with dramatic moments. Sometimes it's subtle—the loss of a dream, a relationship that changed, a version of life I thought I'd have by now.

MY EVERYDAY LIFE

These losses don't always make sense to others, so I hold them close, processing them in my own time.

Some nights, I sit with my thoughts longer than I should. I stare at the ceiling, replaying conversations, imagining different outcomes. I wonder how much of life is shaped by the choices we make and how much is shaped by the things we couldn't control. Behind closed doors, there's no pressure to be certain. Uncertainty is allowed to exist here.

I've learned that healing happens in private long before it shows up in public. The world may see confidence, but behind closed doors there were moments of doubt, prayer, journaling, and quiet resilience. Strength doesn't always roar. Sometimes it whispers, Just get through tonight.

There are days when my home feels like a sanctuary and days when it feels like a mirror, reflecting parts of myself I'm not ready to face. Both experiences matter. Both teach me something. I'm learning not to rush my emotional process just to appear put together.

Behind closed doors is where I make promises to myself. Some I keep. Some I break. But the act of making them reminds me that I still believe in growth. That I haven't given up on becoming better, softer, more honest.

I've also learned that rest is not laziness. That saying no is sometimes an act of self-respect. That I don't owe everyone access to my inner world. These lessons didn't come easily. They were learned through exhaustion, disappointment, and moments of emotional burnout.

When I step back into the world, I carry pieces of what I've processed in private. Not everything—some things are just for me. But enough to move forward with intention. Enough to remind myself that the life I live behind closed doors is just as important as the one others see.

Because that's where the real work happens. That's where I heal, reflect, fall apart, rebuild, and prepare to face another day.

And when the door closes again, I know I'll be safe to be exactly who I am.

Chapter 3
The Woman in the Mirror

The woman in the mirror has changed over the years, and not just in ways that time makes obvious. She has changed in her eyes, in her posture, in the way she holds herself when she thinks no one is looking. There was a time when I avoided meeting her gaze for too long. It felt easier to glance quickly and move on, pretending I didn't see the questions staring back at me.

Now, I linger.

The mirror has become a place of reckoning. It doesn't lie, but it also doesn't judge. It reflects what is, not what should be. Some mornings, I look at myself and feel proud. Other mornings, I see exhaustion, disappointment, or uncertainty written across my face. Both versions are real. Both deserve acknowledgment.

As an African American woman, my relationship with my reflection has been shaped by more than personal insecurities. It has been shaped by a world that often tells us who we should be before asking who we are. Beauty standards that never quite included us.

Expectations that demanded strength but discouraged softness. Messages that praised resilience while ignoring the cost of carrying it.

Growing up, I learned early how to assess myself through someone else's lens. Was my hair "acceptable"? Was my body too much or not enough? Was my voice too strong, my presence too noticeable? I learned to critique myself before anyone else could. It felt like protection at the time. In reality, it was survival disguised as self-awareness.

The woman in the mirror remembers those lessons, even now. She remembers shrinking in spaces where she should have expanded. She remembers smiling through discomfort to keep the peace. She remembers apologizing for emotions that were justified. Those memories show up in subtle ways—in the tension in my shoulders, in the hesitation before speaking my truth.

But the woman in the mirror has also learned.

She has learned that confidence isn't loud. It doesn't always announce itself with bold declarations or flawless appearances. Sometimes confidence is simply

MY EVERYDAY LIFE

standing still and refusing to look away. Sometimes it's saying, This is me, without adding an explanation.

There was a time when I believed self-love would arrive all at once, like a final destination. I imagined waking up one day fully comfortable in my skin, untouched by doubt. That day never came. Instead, self-love arrived in fragments—small decisions, quiet affirmations, moments of choosing myself even when it felt unfamiliar.

The mirror witnessed those moments. It saw me learning to speak more gently to myself. It saw me stop criticizing my reflection for things I could not change. It saw me begin to appreciate the body that has carried me through every chapter of my life. This body has held joy, grief, stress, laughter, and survival. It deserves respect, not punishment.

Some days, the woman in the mirror looks tired. And I let her be. I no longer demand perfection from a woman who has done her best with what she had. Rest, I've learned, is not something you earn—it's something you allow. The mirror reminds me of that when I see softness replacing tension, acceptance replacing resistance.

The mirror is also where I confront identity. Who am I beyond the roles I play? Beyond what I provide, fix, or hold together? The woman staring back at me doesn't exist only to serve others. She has dreams, boundaries, and desires that deserve attention. Acknowledging that truth has been uncomfortable, but necessary.

I've spent years being everything for everyone else. The mirror forced me to ask whether I was being anything for myself. That question didn't come with immediate answers. It came with discomfort. With guilt. With fear of disappointing people who were used to my constant availability.

But growth rarely feels polite.

The woman in the mirror has started setting boundaries. She has learned that saying no doesn't make her selfish—it makes her honest. She has learned that protecting her peace is not a betrayal of love. These lessons are still settling in. Some days, they sit heavy. Other days, they feel liberating.

I've also had to unlearn the idea that strength means silence. The mirror has watched me practice speaking up, even when my voice trembles. It has watched me choose truth over comfort, authenticity over

MY EVERYDAY LIFE

approval. Those choices don't always feel rewarding in the moment, but they build something deeper—self-trust.

There is grief in the mirror too. Grief for the woman I once was, who didn't know she deserved more. Grief for the years spent doubting myself, waiting for permission that was never required. I honor that grief now. It deserves space, not dismissal.

And there is pride. Quiet, steady pride. Pride in surviving things that could have broken me. Pride in continuing to show up, even when the path forward wasn't clear. Pride in becoming a woman who listens to her inner voice instead of silencing it.

The mirror doesn't demand that I love everything I see. It only asks that I see myself fully. That I acknowledge complexity instead of chasing perfection. The woman in the mirror is layered—strong and tender, confident and uncertain, healing and still learning.

I no longer rush past her.

Instead, I greet her. Some mornings with kindness, some mornings with patience. I remind her that she is allowed to take up space. That her story is still unfolding. That becoming is not a failure—it's a process.

The woman in the mirror is not finished. She is evolving, shedding expectations that no longer fit, stepping into herself with cautious courage. And every day, she looks back at me, silently asking the same thing:

Will you stand by me today?

And most days now, my answer is yes.

Chapter 4
Lessons I Learned the Hard Way

Some lessons come gently, like advice passed down from someone who wants to protect you. Others arrive without warning, wrapped in disappointment, loss, or pain. Those are the lessons I learned the hard way—the ones that stayed with me because they cost me something.

For a long time, I believed that if I did the right thing, things would turn out right. I believed effort guaranteed outcomes, loyalty guaranteed reciprocity, and patience guaranteed reward. That belief shaped many of my early decisions. It made me generous with my time, forgiving to a fault, and willing to stay in situations longer than I should have.

Life taught me otherwise.

One of the hardest lessons I learned was that good intentions don't always protect you from harm. You can show up with love and honesty and still be misunderstood. You can give your best and still be met with disappointment. Accepting that truth was painful, because it forced me to let go of the illusion of control.

I learned that people don't always treat you the way you treat them. That lesson hurt deeply, especially as someone who values loyalty. I stayed in relationships—romantic, familial, and platonic—hoping that consistency would eventually be returned. I told myself that if I just explained myself better, loved harder, or waited longer, things would change.

Sometimes they didn't.

Walking away was one of the hardest lessons of all. I was taught that endurance was strength, that staying was admirable. But there's a difference between perseverance and self-abandonment. I learned that lesson slowly, through exhaustion and quiet resentment. I learned it when my body started reacting before my mind caught up—tight chest, constant fatigue, emotional numbness.

Another lesson came in the form of silence. I learned that speaking up late often comes from staying quiet too long. I avoided conflict to keep peace, but peace built on silence isn't peace at all. It's avoidance. I

MY EVERYDAY LIFE

learned that my voice mattered, even if it shook. Especially if it shook.

Being an African American woman added layers to these lessons. There's often pressure to be agreeable, to be strong without complaint, to avoid being labeled as difficult. I internalized that pressure. I minimized my needs, softened my truths, and second-guessed my instincts. The cost of that came later, in moments when I realized I had abandoned myself to make others comfortable.

I learned that boundaries aren't walls—they're doors with locks. They decide who gets access and how much. At first, setting boundaries felt cruel. I worried about hurting people, being misunderstood, or losing relationships. What I didn't realize was that relationships that require self-erasure aren't healthy to begin with.

I also learned that rest is essential, not optional. Burnout taught me that lesson when I refused to listen earlier. I wore exhaustion like a badge of honor, believing productivity equaled worth. It took emotional and physical depletion to show me that rest is an act of respect toward myself.

Some lessons came through failure. Not dramatic failure, but quiet ones—missed opportunities, choices that didn't lead where I hoped, plans that fell apart. I learned that failure doesn't mean you're incapable; it means you're human. It means you tried. Learning to forgive myself for not knowing what I couldn't have known was a lesson I resisted, but needed.

Trust was another lesson learned painfully. I learned that trust should be built, not rushed. That intuition often speaks before logic catches up. I learned to listen when something feels off instead of explaining it away. Ignoring my instincts had consequences, and I don't ignore them anymore.

I learned that healing isn't linear. You don't "get over" things and move on neatly. Some days you feel strong and whole; other days old wounds ache unexpectedly. Healing looks messy because it is honest. Accepting that stopped me from feeling like I was failing at progress.

There were lessons about love, too. I learned that love should feel safe, not confusing. That consistency matters more than grand gestures. That love doesn't require you to shrink, perform, or beg. These lessons didn't come easily. They came through disappointment and reflection, through choosing myself when it would have been easier not to.

One of the most important lessons I learned was that I am allowed to change. The version of me who made certain choices did so with the knowledge she had at the time. I no longer shame her for that. Growth requires compassion for who you were, not punishment.

Hard lessons leave marks, but they also leave wisdom. They shape discernment. They teach you what to walk away from, what to hold onto, and what to protect fiercely. I don't regret learning them, even though I wish they hadn't been so painful.

Because those lessons made me more honest with myself. More aware. More intentional. They taught me that my peace matters. That my time matters. That I matter.

And while I didn't ask for many of those lessons, I carry them now with gratitude—not because they hurt, but because they taught me how to live with more clarity and self-respect.

Part II

Everyday Realities

Chapter 5
Balancing It All

Balance is a word people use casually, as if it's something you can easily achieve once you organize your schedule or learn how to say no. For me, balance has never been a steady state. It has always been a negotiation—between what's needed and what's possible, between who I am and who I'm expected to be.

Some days, balancing it all feels like standing on one foot, arms stretched wide, hoping not to fall. Other days, it feels like controlled movement, like I've finally found my rhythm. But most days, it's somewhere in between—messy, imperfect, and constantly shifting.

As an African American woman, I learned early how to juggle responsibilities. It was never presented as a choice; it was simply what needed to be done. Show up. Handle it. Keep going. I watched the women before me carry families, jobs, emotions, and expectations with quiet determination. Their strength inspired me, but it also set a standard I felt pressured to live up to.

I became someone others relied on. The dependable one. The strong one. The one who could handle it. At first, that role felt empowering. Being needed gave me purpose. But over time, it became heavy. I didn't realize how rarely I asked myself what I needed because I was so focused on meeting everyone else's expectations.

Balancing work and personal life has been one of my greatest challenges. There were times when work demanded more than I had to give, and I gave it anyway. I stayed late, pushed through exhaustion, and told myself rest could wait. I convinced myself that slowing down meant falling behind. What I didn't see at the time was how much of myself I was leaving behind in the process.

At home, the balance looked different but felt just as heavy. Emotional labor doesn't come with a schedule. It shows up in listening, comforting, remembering, anticipating needs before they're spoken. It's the invisible work that keeps relationships afloat. I carried that too, often without realizing how draining it could be.

There were moments when I felt stretched thin—when every area of my life needed attention at the same time. Those moments taught me that balance isn't about doing everything well. It's about deciding what matters most right now. And that decision changes.

I've had to learn that I cannot be fully present everywhere all the time. Something will always require compromise. Accepting that truth was difficult because it challenged my belief that I could manage everything if I just tried harder. The truth is, trying harder isn't always the answer. Sometimes trying differently is.

Learning to ask for help was part of finding balance. That didn't come naturally to me. I was used to being the helper, not the one asking. I worried about being seen as weak or incapable. But carrying everything alone was costing me my peace. Asking for support became an act of self-respect.

I also had to redefine success. For a long time, success meant achievement—goals met, responsibilities handled, boxes checked. But that definition left little room for rest, joy, or presence. I began to ask myself what success would look like if my well-being mattered just as much as my productivity.

Some days, success looks like completing a long to-do list. Other days, it looks like choosing rest over obligation. Balance doesn't always look impressive from the outside, but it feels honest on the inside.

I've learned to release the guilt that comes with prioritizing myself. That guilt was loud at first, fueled by years of conditioning that taught me self-sacrifice was the highest virtue. But sacrificing myself was not sustainable. Balance required boundaries, and boundaries required courage.

There were relationships that had to change for balance to exist. Conversations that had to be had. Expectations that needed to be adjusted. Not everyone understood those changes, and that was difficult. But balance doesn't come from being understood by everyone—it comes from being aligned with yourself.

I've also learned to listen to my body. It speaks in ways my mind sometimes ignores. Fatigue, tension, and restlessness are signals, not inconveniences. Honoring those signals became part of maintaining balance. Ignoring them always led to burnout.

Balancing it all also means accepting seasons. There are seasons of growth, seasons of rest, seasons of survival. Expecting myself to operate the same way in

MY EVERYDAY LIFE

every season was unrealistic. Giving myself permission to move with the rhythm of my life changed everything.

There are still days when balance feels out of reach. Days when things pile up and I feel overwhelmed. On those days, I remind myself that balance isn't about perfection. It's about awareness. It's about checking in and adjusting as needed.

I'm learning that balance is personal. What works for someone else may not work for me. And that's okay. I no longer chase someone else's version of a well-lived life. I'm building my own, one decision at a time.

Balancing it all has taught me patience—with my circumstances, with others, and with myself. It has taught me that I don't have to carry everything at once. That I am allowed to set things down. That my worth isn't tied to how much I can endure.

I'm still learning. Still adjusting. Still finding my footing. But now, I move with intention instead of obligation. With awareness instead of pressure. And that, to me, feels like balance.

Chapter 6
Love, Family, and Expectations

Love and family are often spoken about as if they are simple, comforting things—sources of unconditional support and belonging. For me, love and family have always been layered. Full of warmth, yes, but also expectation. Full of connection, but also responsibility. Navigating that complexity has shaped much of who I am.

Family was my first classroom. It taught me how to love, how to adapt, and how to survive. It also taught me how to prioritize others before myself. I learned early that being dependable mattered. That showing up mattered. That holding things together was often praised more than expressing how you felt while doing it.

I loved my family deeply, and still do. That love was never in question. But love, when mixed with expectation, can become heavy. There were unspoken rules—about who I should be, how I should act, what I should tolerate. I followed those rules for a long time because I didn't know there were alternatives.

MY EVERYDAY LIFE

As an African American woman, family expectations carried cultural weight. Strength was assumed. Sacrifice was expected. Emotional endurance was admired. I watched women in my family give endlessly, often without pause. I absorbed that as normal. I didn't question whether it was fair. I just learned to do the same.

Love, in that context, became something I expressed through action more than words. I showed love by being present, by helping, by putting my needs last. That pattern followed me into other relationships too. Romantic relationships, friendships—anywhere love existed, expectation wasn't far behind.

I wanted to be the one people could count on. The one who didn't complain. The one who handled things quietly. At first, that identity felt meaningful. Over time, it became exhausting. I didn't realize how much of myself I was giving away in the name of love.

Family dynamics don't always leave room for honesty. Sometimes truth feels disruptive. I learned to soften my words, to choose peace over expression. I told myself it was maturity. In reality, it was fear—fear of conflict, fear of disappointing people I cared about, fear of being seen as ungrateful.

Love asked things of me that I didn't know how to refuse.

There were moments when I felt torn between who I was becoming and who my family expected me to remain. Growth doesn't always fit neatly into old roles. As I began to change—setting boundaries, expressing needs, choosing myself—tension followed. Not everyone understood that my evolution wasn't rejection. It was survival.

Romantic love brought its own lessons. I learned how easily expectations form when love isn't grounded in mutual understanding. I learned that love shouldn't require me to constantly prove my worth or shrink my voice. Some relationships taught me what love wasn't before I could recognize what it was.

I gave my heart generously, sometimes to people who didn't know how to hold it. I confused attention with care, effort with intention. I stayed longer than I should have, believing love meant endurance. Letting go challenged everything I thought I knew about commitment.

MY EVERYDAY LIFE

Family expectations didn't always support those lessons. Sometimes love was framed as patience at all costs. Forgiveness without accountability. Staying for the sake of appearance or history. I had to unlearn those messages slowly, carefully, and often painfully.

There came a moment when I realized love should feel safe. Not perfect—but safe. Safe to speak. Safe to rest. Safe to be fully myself. That realization changed how I approached every relationship in my life.

Setting boundaries with family was one of the hardest things I've ever done. It felt unnatural, almost wrong. I worried about being misunderstood. I worried about guilt. I worried about losing connection. But what I was losing already—peace, authenticity, emotional safety—mattered too.

Boundaries didn't erase love. They redefined it.

I began to understand that loving someone doesn't mean carrying their expectations at the expense of my well-being. It means showing up honestly, even when that honesty is uncomfortable. It means choosing relationships that allow growth instead of resisting it.

There were difficult conversations. Awkward silences. Moments of doubt. But there was also relief. Freedom. Space to breathe. Space to be myself without constant explanation.

I've learned that family doesn't always mean agreement. Love doesn't always mean closeness. Sometimes love means distance. Sometimes it means redefining roles. Sometimes it means choosing peace over familiarity.

I still carry love for my family deeply. That love has matured. It's no longer rooted in obligation alone. It's rooted in understanding—of who they are and who I am becoming. We are learning each other again, slowly, imperfectly.

Love today feels different. It feels intentional. It feels grounded. It no longer demands that I disappear to keep it alive. And that difference has changed everything.

I no longer measure love by how much I give up. I measure it by how whole I remain.

Chapter 7
The Weight I Carry Silently

There is a weight I carry that most people never see. It doesn't announce itself. It doesn't demand attention. It simply exists—settled quietly in my chest, my shoulders, my thoughts. I've learned how to carry it well, so well that sometimes even I forget it's there until my body reminds me.

Silence has always been my coping mechanism. Not because I didn't have things to say, but because I learned early that not everything needed to be spoken. Some truths felt safer held inside. Some emotions felt too heavy to explain. Over time, silence became habit. And habits, when practiced long enough, begin to feel like identity.

As an African American woman, silence often felt expected. Strength was praised. Endurance admired. Vulnerability misunderstood. I watched women before me carry unimaginable loads without complaint, and I learned that this was what resilience looked like. I didn't question whether that strength came at a cost. I just inherited it.

The weight I carry is made up of many things. Expectations I didn't choose but accepted anyway. Responsibilities that grew heavier with time. Emotional labor that went unnoticed because I handled it so well. It's made of unspoken grief, postponed dreams, and moments when I needed support but didn't ask for it.

I learned how to smile while carrying heaviness. How to laugh while feeling overwhelmed. How to reassure others while my own doubts went unanswered. The world often rewards that kind of performance. It calls it maturity. It calls it grace. But it rarely asks how much it weighs.

Some of the weight comes from constantly being aware. Aware of how I speak, how I move, how I'm perceived. Aware of stereotypes that linger beneath interactions. Aware of the need to prove myself while pretending I'm not trying to prove anything at all. That awareness never fully rests. It follows me into rooms, conversations, and decisions.

There is also the weight of being needed. Of being the one people turn to for advice, comfort, and stability. I

MY EVERYDAY LIFE

became that person naturally, without realizing how rarely I allowed myself to be the one who leaned. Carrying others emotionally feels noble until you realize you've neglected your own needs.

I carry the weight of holding things together. Of being reliable. Of not letting things fall apart because I'm afraid of what would happen if I did. I've learned how to keep moving even when I'm tired, how to push through discomfort because stopping feels dangerous.

Some nights, the weight settles heavier than usual. It shows up as restlessness, as a mind that won't quiet, as tears that come without explanation. Those nights remind me that carrying things silently doesn't make them disappear. It only postpones their arrival.

There were times when I convinced myself that my weight wasn't heavy enough to matter. That others had it worse. That I should be grateful and quiet. Minimizing my pain felt easier than acknowledging it. But pain doesn't disappear just because you don't name it.

I've learned that silence can protect, but it can also isolate. Carrying everything alone creates distance, even in relationships where love exists. People can't support what they don't know about. I built walls out of quiet and called them independence.

Breaking that pattern has been uncomfortable. Letting people see me when I'm not strong challenges everything I was taught. Vulnerability feels risky when you've learned to survive without it. But I'm learning that strength and softness are not opposites. They can coexist.

The weight I carry has taught me empathy. It's made me attentive to what others don't say. It's taught me how to read between lines, to notice shifts in tone and energy. But it's also taught me the importance of setting the weight down, even if only for a moment.

I'm learning to speak when something is too heavy. To ask for help without apologizing. To trust that being honest doesn't make me weak—it makes me real. These lessons are still settling in. Some days I do better than others.

There are things I still carry quietly. Some experiences are too personal, too layered to share freely. Silence doesn't always mean avoidance. Sometimes it means protection. The difference now is intention. I choose silence instead of defaulting to it.

MY EVERYDAY LIFE

I no longer believe that I have to carry everything alone to be worthy of respect. I no longer believe that my pain has to be invisible to be valid. The weight I carry is real, and acknowledging it has lightened it more than silence ever did.

I am learning to put the weight down when I can. To rest without guilt. To let myself be supported. To accept that I don't have to be strong all the time.

Some days, the weight still returns. But now, I recognize it. I name it. I tend to it with compassion instead of dismissal. And slowly, I am learning that even the strongest shoulders deserve rest.

Chapter 8
Strength in Routine

Routine doesn't sound powerful at first. It sounds ordinary. Predictable. Even boring. But I've learned that routine holds a quiet kind of strength—the kind that keeps you standing when motivation fades and life feels uncertain. In my everyday life, routine has been both a refuge and a foundation.

For a long time, I resisted routine. I associated it with stagnation, with settling. I wanted life to feel inspired, meaningful, intentional. But what I didn't understand then was that inspiration doesn't sustain you on hard days—routine does. Routine shows up when feelings don't. It carries you through when energy is low and clarity is missing.

My routines aren't impressive. They don't belong in productivity books or highlight reels. They are simple, almost invisible to anyone else. Waking up and making my bed. Preparing my morning drink. Moving through the same familiar motions that signal the start of a new day. These acts ground me. They remind me that even when life feels chaotic, there are things I can count on.

As an African American woman, routine has often been a form of survival passed down quietly. I watched women in my life create structure where there was uncertainty. They cooked, cleaned, showed up, and kept going—not because it was glamorous, but because it was necessary. Routine wasn't about comfort; it was about endurance.

I carry that legacy with me, though I've tried to soften it. My routines now are less about survival and more about care. They are small promises I make to myself and keep. In a world that constantly asks me to give, routine is where I give something back to myself.

There is strength in repetition. Doing the same things again and again teaches patience. It builds discipline without demanding perfection. On days when my emotions feel overwhelming, routine becomes an anchor. I don't have to decide what comes next—I simply follow the path I've already laid out.

Routine has also taught me self-trust. When I show up for myself consistently, even in small ways, I reinforce the belief that I matter. That belief wasn't always there. It had to be built slowly, through actions rather than affirmations. Routine gave me that opportunity.

There were seasons when routine was all I had. When motivation disappeared and joy felt distant, routine kept my life from unraveling completely. It didn't fix everything, but it kept me steady enough to endure. Looking back, I see how powerful that was.

I've learned not to underestimate the impact of small, repeated actions. Drinking water. Taking a walk. Writing a few lines in a notebook. These things don't change life overnight, but they change how I move through it. They create momentum where there might otherwise be stagnation.

Routine also creates space for reflection. Familiar patterns leave room for thought. As my hands move through tasks automatically, my mind has space to wander, to process, to heal. Some of my clearest realizations have come during the most ordinary moments—washing dishes, folding clothes, sitting quietly at the end of the day.

There is comfort in knowing what to expect, especially in a world that often feels unpredictable.

MY EVERYDAY LIFE

Routine gives me a sense of control—not over outcomes, but over my own presence. I may not be able to change everything around me, but I can choose how I begin and end my day.

I've had to learn flexibility too. Routine doesn't mean rigidity. Life interrupts. Plans change. Energy shifts. Strength in routine comes from knowing when to adjust without abandoning myself completely. When I miss a day or fall off track, I no longer see it as failure. I simply return when I can.

Some people find routine limiting. For me, it's freeing. It removes unnecessary decisions. It creates stability where I need it most. It reminds me that consistency doesn't have to be loud to be effective.

There's a quiet dignity in showing up for your life every day, even when no one is watching. Even when there's no immediate reward. That dignity lives in routine.

As I've grown, my routines have changed. What once felt necessary may no longer fit. I allow myself to evolve without guilt. Routine isn't meant to trap you—it's meant to support you. When it no longer does, it's okay to redefine it.

Strength in routine doesn't come from perfection. It comes from persistence. From choosing to care for yourself again and again. From building a life that feels manageable, even when it isn't easy.

My routines don't make my life extraordinary. They make it livable. And sometimes, that's more than enough.

In the quiet repetition of everyday moments, I've found stability. In that stability, I've found strength. And in that strength, I continue to move forward—one ordinary day at a time.

Part III

Growth & Reflection

Chapter 9
Healing in My Own Time

Healing is not something I rushed into. It didn't arrive as a clear decision or a dramatic turning point. Instead, it crept into my life slowly, quietly, often when I wasn't looking for it at all. Healing came in moments of exhaustion, in realizations I couldn't ignore anymore, in the understanding that continuing as I was simply wasn't sustainable.

For a long time, I believed healing had a timeline. I thought there was a point where pain expired, where growth was complete, where you could confidently say you were "over it." I learned the hard way that healing doesn't follow schedules or expectations. It moves at its own pace, shaped by readiness rather than desire.

As an African American woman, I felt pressure to heal quickly, quietly, and without inconvenience. Pain was something to manage, not something to sit with. Strength meant moving forward, not lingering. I internalized that belief, pushing myself to be okay before

I actually was. What I didn't realize was that rushing healing only delays it.

There were wounds I avoided because they felt too deep to touch. Old disappointments. Broken trust. Moments where I felt unseen or unheard. I told myself that revisiting those experiences would only reopen wounds I'd worked so hard to close. But avoidance isn't healing—it's postponement.

Healing began when I allowed myself to slow down. When I stopped demanding immediate clarity and allowed confusion to exist. Some days, healing looked like reflection. Other days, it looked like rest. Sometimes it looked like anger, sadness, or grief. I learned that all of it belonged.

I had to confront the idea that healing isn't always comfortable. It doesn't always feel peaceful or empowering. Sometimes it feels raw. Sometimes it feels like loss. Letting go of old identities, old coping mechanisms, and old expectations can feel like grief, even when it's necessary.

Healing in my own time meant learning to listen to myself again. To my body. To my emotions. To the signals I used to ignore. Fatigue became information.

Discomfort became guidance. Silence became space instead of avoidance.

I also learned that healing isn't linear. Progress doesn't move in straight lines. There are days when I feel grounded and strong, and days when old feelings resurface without warning. At first, those moments felt like failure. Now, I understand them as reminders that healing deepens in layers.

Comparison was one of the biggest obstacles to my healing. Watching others move on faster, appear happier, or seem more settled made me question my own progress. I had to learn that healing isn't visible, and it isn't comparable. What works for someone else may not work for me—and that doesn't make my journey wrong.

Some of my healing happened alone. In quiet moments. Through journaling, reflection, and intentional solitude. Other parts of healing happened through conversation—speaking truths I'd held back, allowing myself to be seen, even when it felt uncomfortable. Both were necessary.

Forgiveness became a complicated part of healing. I learned that forgiveness doesn't mean excusing harm or rushing reconciliation. Sometimes forgiveness is internal—a release of resentment so it no longer consumes you. Sometimes it doesn't involve the other person at all.

I also had to forgive myself. For staying too long. For not knowing better. For believing things that weren't true. That self-forgiveness didn't come easily. I had to remind myself that I made decisions based on the information and capacity I had at the time. Compassion toward myself became essential.

Healing in my own time also meant redefining what "better" looked like. Better didn't mean forgetting the past or never feeling pain again. Better meant understanding myself more deeply. It meant responding instead of reacting. It meant choosing peace more often than chaos.

There were moments when I felt pressure to explain my healing to others—to justify why I wasn't ready to move on, why I needed space, why I was changing. Eventually, I realized I didn't owe anyone a timeline or an explanation. Healing is personal. It doesn't require permission.

As I healed, my relationships changed. Some grew stronger. Others faded. That shift was painful, but necessary. Healing often disrupts dynamics built on old versions of yourself. Letting those changes happen without forcing outcomes became part of my growth.

I'm still healing. I don't say that with frustration anymore. I say it with acceptance. Healing isn't something to finish—it's something to tend to. It's an ongoing relationship with yourself.

Some days, healing looks like confidence. Other days, it looks like gentleness. Sometimes it looks like boundaries. Sometimes it looks like rest. All of it counts.

Healing in my own time has taught me patience. With myself. With my process. With my life. It has taught me that I don't have to be fixed to be worthy. I don't have to be finished to be whole.

I am learning to trust my pace. To honor where I am instead of rushing toward where I think I should be. Healing is happening, even when it's quiet, even when it's slow.

And that is enough.

Chapter 10
When I Chose Myself

For most of my life, choosing myself felt like something I wasn't allowed to do. It wasn't written anywhere, but it was understood—in the way I was raised, in the expectations placed on me, and in the roles I learned to fill. I learned early how to be dependable, how to be strong, how to put my needs last without calling it sacrifice. I called it love. I called it responsibility. I called it being a good woman.

But deep down, I was tired.

Not the kind of tired sleep could fix, but the kind that settles into your spirit when you've been living for everyone else for too long. I didn't notice it at first. I just felt disconnected from myself, like I was moving through my days on autopilot, doing what needed to be done but rarely asking how I was doing.

Choosing myself wasn't a sudden decision. It was a slow realization that something had to change. I started noticing how often I ignored my own feelings to keep the peace. How often I said yes when my heart was screaming no. How often I minimized my needs so others wouldn't feel uncomfortable.

I told myself that this was just how life was. That everyone felt this way. That wanting more peace or more space made me selfish. But the truth was, I wasn't choosing selflessness—I was choosing silence. And silence was costing me parts of myself I didn't even realize I was losing.

The moment I truly chose myself didn't come with applause or validation. It came with discomfort. With guilt. With fear of disappointing people who were used to me always being available, always understanding, always accommodating. Choosing myself meant redefining who I was to others—and to myself.

I remember the first time I honored my own boundary without explaining it away. I didn't overtalk. I didn't apologize. I simply stood firm. My hands were shaking, but my spirit felt steady. That was new for me. Empowering. Terrifying. Necessary.

Choosing myself meant learning that rest is not laziness. That saying no does not make me unkind. That protecting my peace is not a betrayal of love. It meant unlearning the belief that my worth was tied to how much I could endure.

As an African American woman, the pressure to be strong runs deep. Strength is praised, expected, and often demanded. But no one talks enough about how heavy that strength can become when it's never balanced with softness. I had been strong for so long that I forgot how to be gentle with myself.

Choosing myself meant allowing vulnerability. It meant admitting when I was overwhelmed. It meant asking for help instead of wearing exhaustion like a badge of honor. It meant giving myself permission to feel without immediately trying to fix or justify those feelings.

There were relationships that shifted when I chose myself. Some people understood. Some didn't. Some were supportive. Some pulled away. That was one of the hardest parts—accepting that choosing myself might mean outgrowing certain dynamics. But I learned that not everyone who benefits from your silence will celebrate your voice.

I didn't stop caring about others when I chose myself. I simply stopped abandoning myself in the process. I learned that I could love deeply and still have limits. That I could be kind and still be firm. That I could show up without losing myself.

Choosing myself also meant redefining my priorities. I started paying attention to what drained me and what nourished me. I became more intentional with my time, my energy, and my emotional investment. I stopped forcing myself into spaces where I felt unseen or unappreciated.

This choice changed how I moved through my everyday life. I woke up more aware. More honest. More connected to myself. I listened to my intuition instead of second-guessing it. I trusted myself to know what I needed—even when that need was rest, space, or solitude.

There were days when choosing myself felt lonely. Growth often does. But even in those moments, I felt a deeper sense of alignment. A quiet confidence that came from knowing I was finally standing on my own side.

Choosing myself didn't solve all my problems. Life didn't suddenly become easy. But it became more authentic. I stopped living on autopilot and started living with intention. I stopped shrinking and started taking up the space I deserved.

MY EVERYDAY LIFE

Looking back, I realize that choosing myself wasn't a single decision—it was a commitment. A daily practice. A promise I made to honor who I am and who I am becoming. Some days I do it better than others. But I no longer ignore myself the way I once did.

When I chose myself, I chose healing. I chose honesty. I chose peace over performance. And that choice continues to shape my everyday life in ways I am still discovering.

Choosing myself wasn't the end of who I was—it was the beginning of who I am.

Chapter 11
Faith, Hope, and Resilience

Faith didn't always look the way I thought it would in my life. I used to believe faith was loud—full of certainty, confidence, and unwavering belief. I thought it meant having all the answers or never doubting the path ahead. But my faith was built differently. It was quieter. More fragile at times. And yet, stronger than I ever imagined.

There were seasons when faith was the only thing holding me together. Not the kind that erased my struggles, but the kind that helped me endure them. The kind that whispered, keep going, even when I didn't know where I was headed.

Hope, too, came in waves. Some days it felt close enough to touch. Other days it felt distant, like something meant for other people. I learned that hope isn't always optimism. Sometimes it's simply the decision not to give up. Sometimes it's getting out of bed when your heart feels heavy. Sometimes it's believing that your current situation is not your final destination.

MY EVERYDAY LIFE

Resilience was something I carried long before I knew the word for it. It lived in my ability to adapt, to survive, to keep moving forward even when life felt unfair. As an African American woman, resilience was modeled to me early—through generations of women who endured hardship with grace, who carried families, faith, and futures on their shoulders without complaint.

But resilience came at a cost.

For a long time, I thought resilience meant never breaking. Never needing help. Never admitting weakness. I didn't realize that true resilience also includes rest, reflection, and healing. It includes knowing when to pause instead of pushing through. It includes trusting that you don't have to do everything alone.

Faith taught me that I didn't have to understand everything to trust that there was purpose in my journey. It taught me that unanswered prayers weren't always denials—sometimes they were redirections. I began to see that delays didn't mean abandonment, and struggles didn't mean failure.

Hope began to feel less like a destination and more like a practice. I practiced hope by choosing gratitude, even on hard days. I practiced hope by speaking kindly to myself when self-doubt crept in. I practiced hope by imagining a future that felt peaceful instead of just productive.

There were moments when I questioned everything—my choices, my strength, my worth. In those moments, faith didn't show up as certainty. It showed up as endurance. As the ability to keep trusting even when clarity was missing. As the courage to believe that something better could exist beyond what I could currently see.

Resilience, I learned, is not about how much you can handle—it's about how deeply you can heal. It's about allowing yourself to be changed by your experiences rather than hardened by them. It's about carrying your story with honesty instead of shame.

I began to understand that my faith didn't require perfection. It required presence. It required honesty. It required a willingness to show up as I was, not as I thought I should be. That realization brought me peace.

Hope became more grounded. Less about wishing and more about trusting the process. I stopped rushing my healing. I stopped comparing my journey to others. I allowed myself to move at my own pace, knowing that growth is not a competition.

Resilience showed itself in small ways—choosing rest, setting boundaries, asking for help, forgiving myself. These acts didn't look heroic, but they were transformative. They allowed me to live more fully instead of merely surviving.

There were days when all three—faith, hope, and resilience—felt stretched thin. On those days, I learned that it was enough to simply keep breathing. Enough to keep believing that tomorrow could be different. Enough to trust that I was not alone, even when I felt lonely.

Faith reminded me that my story had meaning beyond my struggles. Hope reminded me that my future was still unfolding. Resilience reminded me that I had already survived more than I once thought possible.

Together, they became the foundation of my everyday life. Not as abstract ideas, but as lived experiences. As quiet companions that walked with me through uncertainty, growth, and healing.

I am still learning what faith looks like for me. Still redefining hope. Still practicing resilience in healthier ways. But I no longer doubt their presence in my life. They have carried me through seasons I never imagined I would survive.

And because of them, I stand here—still growing, still believing, still moving forward—with a heart that knows strength and a spirit that refuses to give up.

Faith, hope, and resilience are not just parts of my story.
They are the reason I am still telling it.

Chapter 12
Becoming More Than I Was

There was a time when I believed growth meant leaving my past behind completely. I thought becoming more required forgetting who I once was—her mistakes, her fears, her softness. I didn't want to remember the woman who doubted herself, who stayed quiet too long, who carried guilt for things that were never hers to hold.

But becoming more than I was didn't mean erasing her.
It meant understanding her.

Every version of me played a role in getting me here. The woman who endured. The woman who questioned. The woman who survived things she never talked about. Each one left something behind—wisdom, strength, awareness. I learned that growth is not about replacement; it's about integration.

Becoming more required honesty. I had to be honest about where I had been and where I wanted to go. I had to acknowledge patterns that no longer served me and beliefs that kept me small. That honesty wasn't comfortable, but it was freeing.

For a long time, I limited myself without realizing it. I accepted less because I didn't believe I deserved more. I stayed silent because I feared being misunderstood. I tolerated imbalance because I thought that was just part of life. Growth began the moment I questioned those assumptions.

Becoming more than I was meant raising my standards—not just for others, but for myself. It meant holding myself accountable to the life I wanted to live. I stopped making excuses for my unhappiness and started making space for change.

As an African American woman, becoming more also meant reclaiming my narrative. For too long, I felt defined by expectations—what I should be, how I should act, how much I should carry. I realized that those expectations were not my identity. They were limitations placed on me by a world that often misunderstood my strength.

I began to give myself permission to evolve. To outgrow old roles. To say, This no longer fits me. That permission changed everything. It allowed me to step into new ways of thinking, loving, and living.

Growth didn't come without discomfort. There were moments when I felt uncertain, stretched, and unsure of who I was becoming. But even in those moments, I felt aligned. I knew I was moving forward instead of standing still.

Becoming more meant learning to trust myself. To trust my intuition. To trust my ability to navigate change. I stopped seeking constant validation from others and started listening inward. That shift gave me confidence rooted in self-awareness instead of approval.

I also learned that growth doesn't mean constant motion. Sometimes becoming more means slowing down. Reflecting. Letting things settle. Allowing lessons to take shape before moving on. I stopped rushing my evolution and started honoring its pace.

The woman I am becoming is more intentional. More grounded. More aware of her worth. She doesn't chase what doesn't serve her. She doesn't beg for what should be freely given. She values peace as much as progress.

Becoming more than I was didn't change my past—but it changed how I relate to it. I no longer view my struggles as weaknesses. I see them as evidence of endurance. I see them as chapters that shaped me rather than scars that define me.

There are still days when I reflect on who I used to be. Not with regret, but with compassion. She did the best she could with what she knew at the time. And because of her, I am here—wiser, stronger, and more open to what's possible.

I am not done becoming. Growth is ongoing, and I welcome it. I no longer fear change the way I once did. I understand now that change is not loss—it's expansion.

Becoming more than I was is not about perfection. It's about alignment. It's about living in truth instead of habit. It's about honoring who I am while remaining open to who I can still become.

And as I move forward, I carry this truth with me:
I am not trying to escape my past.
I am building on it.

Becoming more than I was is the quiet, powerful work of choosing growth every day.

PART IV
LOOKING FORWARD

Chapter 13
Gratitude in Small Moments

For a long time, I believed gratitude was something you practiced when life was going well. I thought it belonged to celebrations, answered prayers, and moments of abundance. I didn't realize that gratitude could also live in the ordinary, in the quiet spaces between major events, in the moments that often go unnoticed.

Learning gratitude in small moments changed the way I experienced my everyday life.

It didn't happen all at once. At first, gratitude felt forced, like something I was supposed to feel rather than something I genuinely experienced. But slowly, as I began to pay attention, gratitude softened. It became more natural, more honest. I stopped looking for big reasons to be thankful and started noticing the small ones.

I became grateful for calm mornings, even when they were brief. For moments of laughter that came unexpectedly. For the comfort of familiar routines. These small moments didn't fix everything, but they grounded me. They reminded me that life wasn't only made up of struggles—it was also made up of grace.

Gratitude helped me slow down. It taught me to pause and acknowledge what was present instead of focusing solely on what was missing. I realized how often I rushed through my days, always thinking about what needed to happen next. Gratitude invited me into the now.

As an African American woman, I was taught resilience early. I learned how to push through, how to endure, how to stay strong. Gratitude offered a softer way of living. It allowed me to appreciate my strength without being consumed by struggle. It reminded me that joy and resilience can exist together.

I began to notice beauty in unexpected places. The way sunlight filled a room. The peace of a quiet evening. The comfort of being understood without explanation. These moments didn't demand anything from me. They simply existed, and that was enough.

Gratitude also changed how I viewed challenges. It didn't erase them, but it helped me approach them with a different mindset. I started asking myself what each experience was teaching me instead of focusing only on how difficult it felt. That shift brought clarity and growth.

I learned to be grateful for progress, even when it was slow. For healing, even when it wasn't complete. For lessons, even when they came through discomfort. Gratitude taught me that growth doesn't have to be perfect to be meaningful.

Some days, gratitude looked like acknowledging my effort. Other days, it looked like giving myself permission to rest. It wasn't always about feeling joyful—it was about being aware. Being present. Being honest about what I had and what I needed.

Gratitude deepened my relationships. It helped me appreciate people for who they were instead of who I expected them to be. It allowed me to show up with patience and understanding. It softened my heart and expanded my compassion.

There were moments when gratitude felt difficult—when life felt heavy, uncertain, or unfair. On those days, gratitude was quiet. It showed up as endurance. As trust. As the belief that this moment, too, would pass.

MY EVERYDAY LIFE

I learned that gratitude doesn't require perfection. It requires attention. It asks us to notice the life we are already living instead of waiting for a different one. That realization brought peace.

Gratitude in small moments transformed my everyday life. It reminded me that meaning isn't always found in big achievements—it's found in presence. In awareness. In the willingness to recognize what is good, even when everything isn't.

As I reflect now, I see how these small moments carried me. How they offered balance when life felt overwhelming. How they helped me stay grounded as I continued to grow.

Gratitude didn't change my circumstances, but it changed my perspective. And sometimes, that makes all the difference.

In learning gratitude, I learned how to live more fully.
Not by chasing more—but by honoring what already exists.

Chapter 14
Redefining My Everyday Life

For a long time, I thought my everyday life was something I had to endure rather than appreciate. It felt like a series of responsibilities, routines, and quiet sacrifices strung together without much pause. I didn't see it as something worth documenting, worth honoring, or worth celebrating. It was just life—ordinary, repetitive, and often demanding.

Now, I see it differently.

Redefining my everyday life didn't happen all at once. It happened slowly, through reflection, healing, and the courage to look honestly at who I was becoming. It happened when I stopped measuring my life against unrealistic standards and started paying attention to what actually mattered to me.

I used to believe that significance lived in big moments—achievements, milestones, recognition. I waited for life to feel meaningful, assuming it would arrive once everything was in place. But life doesn't

MY EVERYDAY LIFE

pause for perfection. Meaning doesn't wait for ideal conditions. It lives in the moments we often overlook.

My everyday life is not flashy. It doesn't always feel exciting. But it is mine. And that alone gives it value.

Redefining my life meant redefining success. Success is no longer about how much I can handle or how much I can give away. It's about how present I am in my own life. It's about peace, alignment, and honesty. It's about waking up without the weight of pretending.

As an African American woman, redefining my everyday life also meant questioning the expectations placed on me—spoken and unspoken. Expectations to be endlessly strong. To carry more than my share. To remain composed even when overwhelmed. Letting go of those expectations felt uncomfortable at first, almost like betrayal. But it wasn't betrayal. It was liberation.

I began to ask myself different questions. Not What do I owe? but What do I need? Not How do I look? but How do I feel? Those questions changed the direction of my life more than any external achievement ever could.

My everyday life now includes boundaries. It includes rest without guilt. It includes saying no without apology. It includes choosing myself, even when that choice is misunderstood. These things didn't come naturally. They were learned through trial, error, and a deep desire for peace.

I've learned to honor the quiet victories. Getting through a hard day. Speaking up when it mattered. Letting go when holding on was hurting me. These moments may never be recognized publicly, but they shape who I am just as much as any milestone.

Redefining my everyday life also meant accepting imperfection. Some days are productive. Some days are slow. Some days feel heavy. I no longer label those days as failures. They are part of the rhythm of being human. Balance doesn't mean everything feels good—it means everything is allowed to exist.

I've learned that joy doesn't have to be loud to be real. It can live in small moments—a quiet morning, a deep breath, a sense of relief at the end of the day. I pay attention to those moments now. I let them matter.

There was a time when I felt disconnected from my own life, like I was watching it from the outside.

MY EVERYDAY LIFE

Redefining my everyday life brought me back into myself. It reminded me that my experiences, thoughts, and feelings are worthy of attention.

This book is not about having it all figured out. It's about noticing. About reflecting. About honoring the journey as it unfolds. My everyday life continues to change, and so do I. Growth didn't end with this final chapter—it continues beyond it.

I am still learning how to be gentle with myself. Still learning how to trust my voice. Still learning how to live with intention instead of obligation. That learning is part of my everyday life now too.

If there is one thing I know for certain, it's this: ordinary does not mean insignificant. The life we live every day is the life that shapes us. It deserves care. It deserves honesty. It deserves reflection.

My everyday life is no longer something I rush through. It's something I stand in. Something I acknowledge. Something I respect.

And in redefining it, I have found something I didn't know I was missing—peace.

Closing Reflections

ESSAY
Learning To Be Me Again

    Writing this book required me to slow down in ways I wasn't used to. It asked me to sit with my memories instead of rushing past them, to listen to my own voice without judgment, and to honor experiences I once considered too ordinary to matter. In doing so, I came to understand something deeply important: my everyday life has always been speaking to me. I just wasn't always listening.

    For much of my life, I moved forward without pausing to reflect. I did what was expected of me. I carried responsibilities with quiet determination. I learned how to adapt, how to endure, how to be strong—even when I felt uncertain or tired. I rarely questioned whether the way I was living truly aligned with who I was becoming. Life felt like something I had to manage rather than something I was allowed to experience fully.

    This reflection has changed that.

As I revisited different seasons of my life, I began to see patterns—moments where I silenced myself to maintain peace, times when I put my needs aside to meet expectations, and long stretches where I measured my worth by how much I could handle. At the time, I didn't recognize these patterns as self-abandonment. I thought I was being responsible. Loving. Resilient. But reflection has a way of revealing truths that survival keeps hidden.

What I've learned is that survival is not the same as living.

Living requires presence. It requires intention. It requires honesty—not just with others, but with yourself. And that honesty can be uncomfortable. It can challenge beliefs you've carried for years. It can ask you to let go of identities that once protected you but now limit you.

One of the most powerful lessons this journey has taught me is that strength does not have to look like endurance alone. Strength can look like rest. It can look like asking for help. It can look like choosing yourself even when that choice is misunderstood. I spent so many years believing that being strong meant never breaking, never needing, never slowing down. But strength, I've learned, also lives in softness.

As an African American woman, the expectation to be strong runs deep. It is inherited, modeled, and reinforced by both culture and circumstance. I honor that strength—it carried me through difficult seasons and taught me resilience. But I also recognize now that I am allowed to redefine what strength looks like for me. I am allowed to create a life that includes peace, balance, and joy—not just endurance.

This book is not a collection of dramatic events or extraordinary accomplishments. It is a reflection of ordinary moments—the ones that shape us quietly and persistently. The mornings we wake up unsure but still move forward. The conversations we replay in our minds. The choices we make when no one is watching. These moments matter. They build the foundation of who we are.

I used to underestimate the significance of my everyday life. I thought meaning lived somewhere else—in bigger goals, better timing, or future versions of myself. But meaning has always been here, in the life I am already living. It exists in reflection, in growth, in the courage to acknowledge where I am and where I've been.

Throughout this journey, I've learned that growth is not linear. Healing does not follow a straight path. Some lessons return in new forms, asking to be understood more deeply. Some wounds take time to soften. Some changes happen quietly, without announcement. And that's okay.

I've also learned that choosing myself is not a one-time decision. It is a daily practice. It shows up in the boundaries I set, the rest I allow, and the compassion I extend to myself when I fall short. Choosing myself does not mean I stop caring about others—it means I stop disappearing in the process.

Faith, hope, and resilience have been constant companions in my life, even when I didn't recognize them as such. Faith carried me through uncertainty. Hope reminded me that my story was still unfolding. Resilience helped me rise after moments that could have broken me. Together, they formed a foundation that allowed me to keep going—even when clarity was absent.

Gratitude has also reshaped my perspective. Learning to appreciate small moments taught me how to be present. It reminded me that joy doesn't have to be loud to be real. Sometimes joy is quiet—a deep breath, a calm evening, a sense of peace that settles unexpectedly. These moments are not insignificant. They are life.

As I close this chapter of reflection, I do so with greater self-awareness and gentleness than I had before. I no longer feel the need to rush toward an ideal version of myself. I am learning to respect the version I am becoming. Growth, I've learned, is not about arriving—it's about aligning.

This book does not mark the end of my journey. If anything, it marks a beginning. A commitment to live with more intention, more honesty, and more compassion. A commitment to listen to my own needs and trust my own voice. A commitment to honor my everyday life for what it is—real, evolving, and worthy.

If there is one truth I carry forward, it is this: ordinary does not mean unimportant. The life we live each day is the life that shapes us. It deserves reflection. It deserves care. And it deserves acknowledgment.

I am still becoming. Still learning. Still growing. And that, in itself, is enough.

There is another part of my everyday life that reshaped everything—one I could not ignore or minimize, no matter how hard I tried. Life changed when I began carrying an oxygen tank. When walking no longer felt simple or natural. When my body required assistance in ways I never imagined it would.

At first, I struggled with acceptance. Using a walker felt like a visible announcement of vulnerability. Transitioning from a walker to a rollator, and later to a cane, reminded me daily that my independence looked different now. Each device marked a chapter of adjustment, grief, and resilience. I mourned the ease I once had—the ability to move without planning, to leave the house without calculating energy or breath.

There were moments when I felt exposed. Moments when I felt watched. Moments when I felt reduced to what people could see instead of who I am. Carrying oxygen forced me to slow down in a world that rarely pauses. It required patience with my body and compassion for myself—two things I had not always practiced well.

But it also taught me something powerful: my worth was never tied to how fast I could move or how much I could carry. My life did not lose value because my body changed. It gained depth.

Disability reshaped my days, but it did not take away my purpose. It invited me into a different kind of presence. I became more intentional. More aware of my limits—and more respectful of them. I learned that rest is not weakness and that needing support does not diminish dignity.

Through this journey, I did not walk alone.

My husband, Steve, carries his own battles. He lives with hypertension and faces challenges that require daily awareness and care. Together, we both navigate mental health struggles that demand patience, honesty, and grace. There are days when the weight of it all feels heavy—when disability, health concerns, and emotional exhaustion converge.

And yet, even in that reality, gratitude lives.

I am thankful that we have each other. Thankful that love does not require perfection, only commitment. We understand each other in ways that don't need explanation. We recognize effort even on the days when progress is invisible. We show up—not always with answers, but with presence.

Our lives may not look the way we once imagined, but they are rich with connection. We have learned how to support one another without judgment, how to rest together without guilt, and how to celebrate small victories that others may overlook. In a world that often equates value with productivity, we have learned to value care, patience, and mutual understanding.

I am also deeply grateful for the circle of family and friends who surround us with love. Their support reminds me that independence does not mean isolation. That needing help does not mean failing. That community is not a weakness—it is a blessing.

They see us beyond our limitations. They meet us where we are. They remind us that we are still whole.

Living with disability and mental health challenges has taught me that joy is not reserved for ideal circumstances. Joy can coexist with struggle. Peace can exist alongside uncertainty. Love can thrive even when bodies and minds require extra care.

MY EVERYDAY LIFE

My everyday life now includes oxygen tubing, mobility aids, medication schedules, and intentional pacing. But it also includes laughter, shared understanding, and moments of quiet gratitude. It includes love that adapts, hope that persists, and faith that remains steady even when the path is unclear.

This chapter of my life has required surrender—not resignation, but acceptance. Acceptance that life changes. That bodies change. That strength must be redefined again and again. And in that acceptance, I have found something unexpected: peace.

I am grateful not because life is easy, but because it is shared. Because even in limitation, there is love. Even in struggle, there is connection. Even in uncertainty, there is meaning.

And that, too, is part of my everyday life—worthy of reflection, worthy of honor, and worthy of gratitude.

POEM
Still Becoming

I used to believe life would explain itself to me,
that one day everything would make sense
and I would finally feel finished.

But life didn't come that way.

It came quietly—
in mornings I pushed through,
in nights I prayed silently,
in lessons learned through living
instead of planning.

I am made of ordinary days
woven together by faith,
by tears I didn't always share,
by strength I learned to carry
and gentleness I am still learning to allow.

I am not behind.
I am not unfinished.
I am not lacking.

I am still becoming.

MY EVERYDAY LIFE

I honor the woman I was
when I didn't know how strong I was.
I honor the woman I am
for choosing growth, honesty, and peace.
And I honor the woman I am becoming—
patient, grounded, and more aware of her worth.

This book is not the end of my story.
It is a pause.
A breath.
A reminder that my everyday life—
in all its quiet moments—
has meaning.

And so I move forward,
grateful for where I've been,
present with where I am,
and hopeful for what is still unfolding.

I am still becoming.
And that is enough.

God, I give myself to you, and

I lift up my husband, Steve Robertson, to You too.
Thank You for his life, his heart, and the love we share.

I ask You now to place Your healing hands over him.
Strengthen his body where it feels weak.
Restore his health where it has been challenged.
Cover him with protection, peace, and renewal.

Ease his mind and calm his spirit.
Replace any pain, fear, or discomfort
with strength, reassurance, and hope.

Lord, bless our marriage.
Let our home be filled with love, patience, and joy.
Teach us to communicate with kindness
and to choose each other even on difficult days.

Remove stress and worry from our hearts.
Help us to laugh freely, love deeply,
and grow stronger together.

May our happiness be rooted in faith,
our love grounded in respect,
and our future guided by Your grace.

Thank You for covering Steve,
for sustaining us both,
and for blessing our union with peace and joy.

Amen.

THE ART & ARTIST

THE BOOK

What does everyday life look like when your body changes . . . but your spirit refuses to disappear?

In **MY EVERYDAY LIFE**, Latisha Ann Jefferson-Robertson offers a deeply honest, tender, and powerful reflection on living with disability, chronic illness, and mental health challenges while holding onto love, dignity, and gratitude in the small moments.

As an American woman navigating aboriginal life with an oxygen tank, mobility aids including a walker, rollator, and cane, Latisha shares what it means to adapt without surrendering identity. She writes candidly about the emotional weight of visibility, the quiet grief of lost independence, and the courage it takes to redefine strength.

This memoir also honors marriage under pressure. Latisha and her husband, Steve, both face health challenges — including hypertension and diabetes — yet choose each other daily. Their story is not about perfection, but partnership. Not about overcoming disability, but living fully within it.

With compassion and clarity, Latisha reflects on:
- Disability and dignity in everyday life
- Mental health and emotional resilience
- Marriage, caregiving, and mutual support
- Faith, gratitude, and self-acceptance
- The power of community, family, and chosen support

This is not a story of inspiration for inspiration's sake. It is a story of **truth** — written for disabled readers who rarely see themselves reflected honestly, for caregivers seeking understanding, and for anyone learning how to live gently in a demanding world.

MY EVERYDAY LIFE is Latisha Jefferson-Robertson's fifth book. It was released in January 2026 with assistance from BePublished.org, continuing her commitment to storytelling that affirms lived experience and centers stories of truth too often overlooked.

This book does not ask you to be strong all the time. It invites you to be present. And, it reminds you that you are not alone.

This book is written in solidarity with the disabled community, chronic illness warriors, caregivers, and loved ones who walk beside them. Your life matters. Your pace matters. Your story matters.

Available as an eBook for $5.95, **MY EVERYDAY LIFE** by Latisha Jefferson-Robertson may also be purchased worldwide as a paperback for $14.95 from bricks-and-mortar and online book retailers including your local bookstore and Amazon.com.

THE AUTHOR / DESIGNER

Latisha A. Jefferson-Robertson, a Mississippi native, is an accomplished entrepreneur and celebrated vocalist who performed at Carnegie Hall while a teen member of an award-winning choir at a school in Jackson, Mississippi.

The former Atlanta resident is the author of

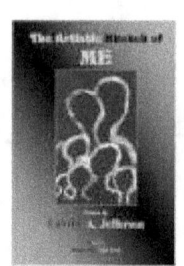

The Artistic Sketch Of Me (a mini-collection of selected poetry published in 2009). A decade later, in 2019, she released her second book titled **This Kindred Heart of Mine** – which  also included prose. The following year, in 202, Latisha wrote **What A Day! What A Day!** one evening in February when  challenged to complete a book in 24 hours. The professional proofreader for BePublished.org rose to the challenge!

Latisha wrote her fourth book the same way,  alongside her husband, author Steve Robertson, in February 2025 – releasing **Kids Gone Wild** the same week her husband's debut **The Importance Of Your Life** was released worldwide by BePublished.org in March 2025.

On January 6, 2026, she and her husband completed a Book Bang workshop through The Writers Consortium's partnership with BePublished.org -- where she created  their book covers and they each wrote their new books. As a result, her fifth book, **MY EVEERYDAY LIFE**, was released that same month.

When she's not busy volunteering to assist the sick/elderly or tending children, Latisha enjoys spending her free time listening to music, playing

Spades and chess, watching movies, enjoying good food, and spending time with loved ones.

A relative of professional football greats including the legendary Walter "Sweetness" Payton and Lynn Swan, Latisha Jefferson-Robertson is currently working on other projects where her creativity lends itself to jewelry making, writing songs, and learning to use AI to perform songs that teach valuable lessons to children.